COPYRIGHT

30 DAYS TO A NEW YOU

THE ABC'S OF FASTING AND

FINDING YOUR TRUE SELF

DEDICATION

Dear Reader,

I want to assure you that if you've ever felt lost, stuck, or uncertain about your purpose in life, you're not one. I've written this book, "30 Days to a New You: The ABCs of Fasting and Finding Your True Self," with you in mind. Whether you're dealing with self-doubt, negative self-talk, or a lack of direction, this book is meant to serve as an empowering guide and a source of inspiration on your path to personal growth and self-discovery.

Within the pages of this book, you'll find prompts and exercises that will help you retrain your brain and build positive habits to reinforce your true self. I'm grateful for the unwavering support of my family and friends throughout this journey, and I'm honored that you've entrusted me with your time and attention.

y intention is for this book to help you find the clarity and peace that you desire. Thank you for allowing me to be a part of your journey toward a new you.

With love and gratitude,

Lesley

INTRODUCTION

Welcome to 30 Days To A New You. The ABCs Of Fasting and Finding Your True Self. I want to start by saying congratulations on taking this step toward personal growth and self-discovery. I created this journal after facing my own struggles, and I wanted to share this journey with you. Remember, your struggles might look different from someone else's but that doesn't make them any less valid.

This process is simple, but it requires your commitment and consistency. When I started this journey, I realized that my mind became clearer and I had more room for joy and love. I felt more empowered and in control of my life.

This process is not a cure-all but a step towards attracting positive energy and connections.

Each letter in the alphabet represents a prompt for you to reflect on your thoughts and feelings. For example, "A" could represent analyzing comments or situations, and for the next 30 days, you could commit to not over-analyzing them. "P" could represent pain for the next 30 days. You could commit to not talking about anything that brings pain in your life.

Remember to end each sentence with what you will do to reinforce your positive thinking and new shift of thinking. This is a wonderful moment that is all thanks to you saying and agreeing that you are ready to take control simply by letting it all go.

Don't feel pressured to stick to each alphabet, and you could stop at the last letter if you feel satisfied. The bigger idea is to retrain Your brain on how you handle addressing or overthink things that take away your joy, so relax, kick back, and remind yourself of your affirmations and commitments during the day. You will be amazed at the positive changes that will come your way.

FOR THE NEXT 30 DAYS I WILL NOT EXPEND ENERGY O ENGAGE WITH

For example, "A": For the next 30 Days, I will fast not analyze everything that was said; inste trust what I say and find peace instead of overanalyzing conversations.

It is important to always end on a positive note with a plan of action when communicating wha won't do.

FOR THE NEXT 30 DAYS I WILL FAST ___ AND INSTEAD_____

analyzing,
attitudes, apples,
Adam, etc.

DAY_____

FOR THE NEXT 30 DAYS I WILL FAST ___ AND INSTEAD_____

bragging, Betty,
bickering, being,
etc.

DAY_____

FOR THE NEXT 30 DAYS I WILL FAST ___ AND INSTEAD_____

criticizing, comparing, crying over, caring about, etc.

DAY_____

FOR THE NEXT 30 DAYS I WILL FAST ___ AND INSTEAD_____

defending,
doubting, denying,
etc.

DAY____

FOR THE NEXT 30 DAYS I WILL FAST ___ AND INSTEAD_____

excusing, enabling,
engaging, envy,
escape, escalate,
etc.

DAY_____

FOR THE NEXT 30 DAYS I WILL FAST ___ AND INSTEAD_____

faking, friends,
fear, family,
favoring, feeling,
focusing, etc.

DAY_____

_____

_____

_____

_____

_____

_____

_____

_____

_____

_____

_____

_____

FOR THE NEXT 30 DAYS I WILL FAST ___ AND INSTEAD_____

giving, going,
growing, grudges,
gas lighting,
gossiping, etc,

DAY_____

FOR THE NEXT 30 DAYS I WILL FAST ___ AND INSTEAD_____

hitting, hurting,
hearing, having,
hostility, hoping, hobby,
happy, health, etc.

DAY_____

FOR THE NEXT 30 DAYS I WILL FAST ___ AND INSTEAD_____

insisting, insecurity,
idolizing, involving,
including, insulting,
initiating, etc.

DAY_____

FOR THE NEXT 30 DAYS I WILL FAST ___ AND INSTEAD_____

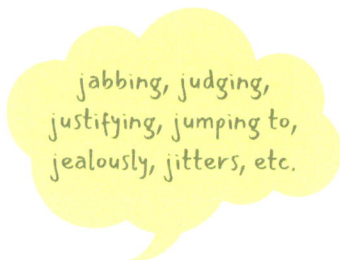

jabbing, judging, justifying, jumping to, jealously, jitters, etc.

DAY_____

FOR THE NEXT 30 DAYS I WILL FAST ___ AND INSTEAD_____

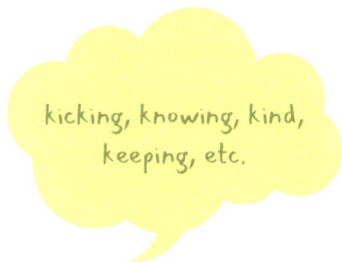

kicking, knowing, kind,
keeping, etc.

DAY____

FOR THE NEXT 30 DAYS I WILL FAST ___ AND INSTEAD_____

lie, lacking, leaving, like, looking, laugh, lazy, love etc.

DAY_____

FOR THE NEXT 30 DAYS I WILL FAST ___ AND INSTEAD_____

manipulate, message,
mind, make, meditate,
maximizing, money,
memory, etc.

DAY____

FOR THE NEXT 30 DAYS I WILL FAST ___ AND INSTEAD_____

never, noticing, nasty,
negotiating, neglecting,
negative, not, etc.

DAY_____

FOR THE NEXT 30 DAYS I WILL FAST ___ AND INSTEAD_____

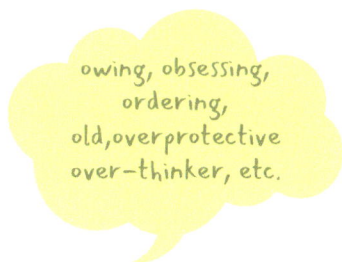

owing, obsessing,
ordering,
old,overprotective
over-thinker, etc.

DAY_____

FOR THE NEXT 30 DAYS I WILL FAST ___ AND INSTEAD_____

problems, pain, people,
petty, panic, perfection,
proud, provide, pick, etc.

DAY_____

_____

_____

_____

_____

_____

_____

_____

_____

_____

_____

_____

_____

FOR THE NEXT 30 DAYS I WILL FAST ___ AND INSTEAD_____

questioning, quiet,
quarrelsome, quick,
quest etc.

DAY_____

FOR THE NEXT 30 DAYS I WILL FAST ___ AND INSTEAD_____

resist, resent, remind,
rule, regret, run,
rectify, remorse, etc.

DAY_____

FOR THE NEXT 30 DAYS I WILL FAST ___ AND INSTEAD_____

shy, seek, stay, speak, surrender, slack, support, suffer, start, selfish, sleep, stop, sassy, etc.

DAY_____

FOR THE NEXT 30 DAYS I WILL FAST ___ AND INSTEAD_____

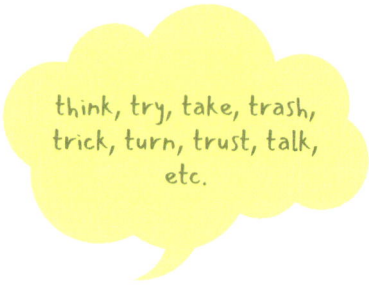

think, try, take, trash,
trick, turn, trust, talk,
etc.

DAY_____

FOR THE NEXT 30 DAYS I WILL FAST ___ AND INSTEAD_____

ugly, underestimate, use, unique, under-appreciate, unpack, under-protect, utter, etc.

DAY_____

FOR THE NEXT 30 DAYS I WILL FAST ___ AND INSTEAD_____

victim, voice, value,
vibes, viscous, vibration,
validation, etc.

DAY_____

FOR THE NEXT 30 DAYS I WILL FAST ___ AND INSTEAD_____

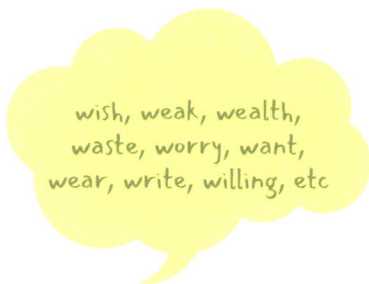

wish, weak, wealth,
waste, worry, want,
wear, write, willing, etc

DAY_____

_____

_____

_____

_____

_____

_____

_____

_____

_____

_____

_____

_____

FOR THE NEXT 30 DAYS I WILL FAST ___ AND INSTEAD_____

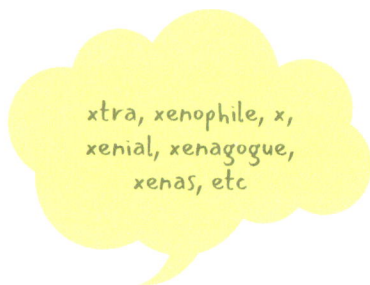

xtra, xenophile, x,
xenial, xenagogue,
xenas, etc

DAY_____

FOR THE NEXT 30 DAYS I WILL FAST ___ AND INSTEAD_____

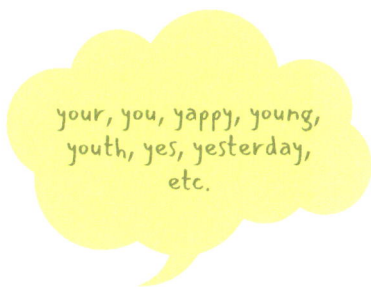

your, you, yappy, young,
youth, yes, yesterday,
etc.

DAY_____

FOR THE NEXT 30 DAYS I WILL FAST ___ AND INSTEAD_____

zoom, zig zag, ZZZ's,
zip, zoo,etc.

DAY_____

I AM STOPPING ___ AND STARTING_____

DAY_____

I AM LEAVING ___ AND RECEIVING_____

DAY_____

I AM SURRENDERING ___ AND ACCEPTING_____

DAY_____

I AM TRUSTING MYSELF TO ___

DAY_____

I FORGIVE MYSELF FOR____

DAY_____

I AM RELEASING____

DAY_____

I DEAL WITH PAIN BY_____

DAY_____

I DEAL WITH DISAPPOINTMENT BY_____

DAY_____

HOLDING ONTO THE PAST HAS____

DAY____

THINKING ABOUT MY FUTURE MAKES ME_____

DAY_____

KNOWING WHAT I KNOW NOW I CAN_____

DAY_____

IF SOMEONE TRIES TO HURT ME OR PROJECT ONTO ME I ____

DAY_____

I WILL NO LONGER GIVE MY POWER AWAY TO ____

Day____

I AM THANKFUL FOR THIS PRESENT MOMENT BECAUSE___

DAY_____

I RESIST COMPARING MYSELF BECAUSE____

DAY____

I HAVE NEVER ADMITTED RESENTING___

DAY_____

WHEN I FEEL STUCK I WILL REMEMBER___

DAY_____

I WAS _____ BUT I AM _____

DAY _____